FIRST EDITION: June 2021
This edition first published in 2021

ISBN 978-1-7777662-0-7 (paperback edition)
ISBN 978-1-7777662-1-4 (hardcover edition)

Kayla Henry
www.kaylahenryonline.com

ACKNOWLEDGEMENTS

David Brookes – Editing
@hillxryl – Illustration

Contents

INTRODUCTION

After my poem entitled "Parrhesia" went viral in May 2021, I saw that the world was crying out for honesty. This realization inspired me to put more of my thoughts on paper. I wanted to express the importance of art, but also the need to step away from it. The way I see it, art has always been a double-edged sword. In one sense, it allows you to present ideas and truths in an accessible way; on the other hand, however, there is a sense of fiction that links itself to it. The main issue I understand is that art can absorb you for long periods of time, muting the real world around you. My poems are built with knowledge and observation, but the formatting and rhymes are what color them as art. As I learn the power of rhetoric, I digest it through my writings and translate it into practical applications. I will not endeavor to tell someone *what* to think. I will, instead, suggest a better method of *how* to think.

Interpret my work as you will, as I intend to spark conversations and critical thinking. I have hope that the lost art of communication will return to us, and I believe that creativity can be the gateway. Let us go back to the time when philosophers would examine complex ideas while promenading in the gardens.

1

NOTE TO THE READER

I hope these poems find you well. They are representations of different times in my life as well as varying cognitive processes. Each poem is an articulation of free expression, and I would like to encourage you to bring liberty to your voice. You will find note pages at the end of this book to store observations and discoveries of your own. Never stop learning.

All the best to you, dear reader. May your mind be open, and the truth be spoken.

With love,

Kayla

Rhymes to Rhetoric

KAYLA HENRY

DEFINE

Words are powerful tools
in communication (out of schools),
freely thinking without rules
which restrict real discoveries.

Define what you mean
before launching it on screen.
Come clean and tell us what you've seen.

Bring clarity to all you say,
as arguments start this way.
Chose to prove or to persuade,
to find truth or to dissuade.

You could dismay—
but is that a noble cause?

SANCTUARY

Under your roof
lies the opportunity
to walk barefoot.
"No shoes, no service"
does not apply here.
Rules aren't necessary.
You make the call:
Put up the sign, or don't.
Condition to suit the scheme
or cultivate a better methodology.
Differentiate between what *is*
and what could be.
Prepare for reality
by acknowledging
that some places
choose frosted windows.

THE LOST ART

The rule of three,
not one without the other:
To observe, question,
and discover.

An innate ability
that we must nurture
to act on logic
after grammar.

Grasp this trio
to disarm
those who use it
for your harm.

VAST

Grateful for everything and the sky in-between.
I can't wait for my subconscious to manifest.
There is always time to understand a concept
if you enable yourself to think critically.

WHAT DID YOU SAY?

Etymology:
The vast history
of characters to words
as the wheel of time turns
and books are burned.

From all corners of the globe
pronunciations unfold.
Letters morphing swiftly,
words shaped in different molds.

Languages built
from shards of others
in a masterpiece
of sounds, shapes and colors.

What a beautiful world
to speak your mind!
The menu is endless,
many options to find.

Under pens or through mouths
understanding is met.
Just remember that words
can be hard to forget.

ALL SPEAK

Freely
candidly
an openness
to speak your mind—
an apology of some kind
for being blunt
and staying bold.

PARRHESIA

It's been like this forever.
This isn't a change of weather.
Freedoms hanging by a thread here
while we binge Netflix and TikTok...

Now, I'm not here to judge you.
I know we're all scared and tired
and we've been so hardwired.
Media fueled the wrong fires.

We're depressed, we're dying
while billionaires are crying
with laughter—
And we're just running faster
away from reality.
Well ... Why wouldn't we?
They've got guns and we've got family.
This isn't conspiracy—
theories have been brought to light
throughout history.
We're in a cave thinking we're free.
Won't go to the light,
it's easier not to see.

Can we go back to dictionaries?
When definitions were clear?
We don't read, we just fear.

Words manipulated we didn't know existed.
Let teachers fix it
so parents can be distant.
Mess with child development.
"Just leave it to the government,"
let them draw our paths
'cause we gave them the pencil.

We can erase this if we face it.
Us against the faces
that convince us drugs
will solve our problems
while they profit from our consumption.

Stop listening to stars and politicians
and begin using intuition,
Discerning fact from fiction.
Stop paying into our addiction
of listening to a system
that's turning us into victims
of our lack of wisdom.

If you don't see it now,
it's okay to be confused,
but don't throw rocks at those who do.
Take a step back and you'll see who
is piloting this ruse:

A bunch of individuals
profiting from your residuals,
putting our money
into propaganda and riot police
instead of into our failing healthcare system.

They've always done this:
saying they need our cash to fix the roads
while they ride private jets and fancy boats.
No wonder we can't stay afloat...

We're right where they want us:
distanced and thoughtless,
avoiding each other
so we can't discuss
what's wrong with this picture.
Instead we write our feelings—
caps lock on with words vomiting
out of our thumbs
without knowledge of real arguing.

Why can't ideas be shared
without ruining friendships and careers?
Just 'cause someone got offended?
Never learned emotional intelligence?
Your feelings have no relevance
in the crusade for truth.

If they gave any credit to the people
we wouldn't have censored information.
We just see one side on every station
pushing separation between each other
so we're too busy judging mothers
who wonder why their kids
are being smothered—
Masks in gym class, call out the other
when he pulls down his mask.
How do they even learn in class?

Ads selling problems not solutions.
Our institutions told us
following was the solution.
'Cause if you think for yourself
"you'll go nowhere with an F."

But I can tell you
the people who came out independent
were the ones who were observant.
I had to unlearn to become present,
and yeah, I'm still working on it,
but I make choices for myself.

This isn't about health.
If it were they'd tell us:

"get your vitamins"
"go for walks whenever you can"
"do sports and eat well"
"have interactions – real human connections"
"raise your kids with healthy immune
systems".

Instead they punish insurrections
that fight for freedom from the infectious
disease that is control.

They swallow us whole.
Keep us indoors.
Special treatment for big-box stores,
but give us fines when we're unsure
what martial law is in place today.
Throw us cheques to stay
on our good side,
keep us lost and afraid
'cause we can't afford
a rising mortgage or rent
since we lost our pay.

It was never gonna be just a few days.

SAYING NO

Silence
Compliance

Synonymous in an upside-down world.

We make up stories to keep ourselves at bay.
Creating realities in our minds
to keep us blind from what is to come.
But we will never know until it happens,
and even so....

BALANCE

I miss the man
who stood tall before adversity
and the woman
who never let him go hungry.

LOOKING OUT

Courage behind a voice.
Cold feet is a choice.
Years of all this noise
bring tears to dreams at night.

There are times to sit
and times to wait
to take it in
and see things straight

but once you do, do not fall back.
As of dawn, progress.
See now the panorama
and then observe the rest.

DECIDE

I could live a sheltered life
or expose myself to strife
but if I take the latter
let it be for what is right.

TO MY FUTURE SELF

A time may come
when I wish I'd been stronger
but I gave in to my hunger
for empty promises and handshakes.
I have swallowed my words
to the point of choking—
all the while hoping
that things would just work out.
Running without purpose
as the path was made so obvious
to distract from tales of lobbyists
who toy with those in power.

No matter where, we're all the same
when life is illustrated as a game.
Winning comforts and empty fame,
the pedestals will never change.

Convinced myself through unjust notions
this was the way of the world
and now little girls live in fear
just as I had all those years.

QUICK, PRESS MUTE!

Genuine roars,
recounting of stories—
What happened to real comedy?

I miss when
truth made us laugh—
but we decided it offends.

Does anyone know
how I missed the vote
for a voice unplugged and free?

QUIET

Sometimes I crave something simpler:
A life off the grid, on a farm, by the lake.
I got used to the babel and energy
of an environment I did not create.

I have stumbled through many a city,
I've valued the community around—
but the peace of mind I truly need
is the quietude out of these towns.

DOG AND TAIL

Wishing on landscapes.
Fountains turned their back on me.
Shooting stars are hard to see
when living under clouds.

Keep me running,
chasing all that's behind.
Dog and tail,
tooth and nail.
Can't get no reward.

Befriend the bus driver;
he doesn't know my name.
Better that way
anyway.

Come and go
'cause he'll never know
I've been sitting here all day
for a nod and a wave.
That's my accolade.

THE BEE

Always working

it's his nature

not preoccupied

by papers

full of purpose

without wasting

hard times come

but never change him.

PEACE

A lookout porch,

twinkling streetlights,

a red-stained wine glass...

Down the street a trill of piano
repeats in practice.

Leave me for a moment to take the picture:
In peace – a perfect still I now carry
in my pocket.

In all the silence I disappear.
My chest is warm, the air is chilled.

The moment you forget you're breathing
you escape to ever-presence.

SHORE OF DREAMERS

Sandcastles in the moonlight turn to stone.
The artist paints the horizon
with strokes of burgundy.

The current's roar cries out to the lonely;
whispers of home from the abyss.

Calling my name as you overflow,
crashing with ghosts of dreamers lost.

Find my tear like the single needle
amongst the hay; invisible but never gone.

NUMB

I long for the sky
but I keep myself tied
down on my luck.

WE'RE SICK

What makes us sick?
Is it airborne, is it quick?
It's much more gradual.
Yes – much more cruel.
Like a man of sound mind
following a fool.

Emptying coffers
through miniscule holes—
eating away at the soles
of your shoes.

The youth of this world?
Their importance is fading.
According to sources:
We're always complaining.

But we are the world—
it's all ours to lose.
Put the few first
and the many you abuse.

31

UNDER THE MATTRESS

Nights are closed for business
so you've got no witnesses.
Take away the face for little kids;
they won't know who mama is.

Pay me off to dull my brain;
couch to bed, you play the queen,
the king, the god, the decider—
I've got my own mind.

Where were you
when cigarettes killed our kind?
Mankind was left behind
so you can drive off, fly off.
Get off to the decline.
You've got no spine.

Thoughtless signatures on paper
while your coffee's still hot.
Don't like when we make money
so now you legalize pot?

Stick your hand in the jar
of ashes you've created,
the stashes you raided
and the mansions you upgraded.
You say *we're* the ones all faded?

You took away our youth:
Automatons from books
that told us broken history—
left reality a mystery—
and now it won't exist 'cause we
all think we screwed each other.

Hate on hate turns us away
from real wars, real enemies.
Too busy pointing fingers.
All the while you still linger
like ghosts or puppeteers
manipulating with fear
as you sit on leather chairs
and tell us we can save the Earth.

While *you* pour money into oil
the princess *and* the pea will spoil.

BRANDED

Interpretations no longer live solely for art.
Seems like anything you say these days
can be misconstrued in part.
If it's at the dinner table
or a simple post on Twitter
you get labeled as something you're not
to sell someone else's theatre.

SOCIAL

Guilt by association;
contrasting friends
don't fit this nation.
They don't like when you interact
with people on the other track.

forNEVER ALONE

You are never alone.
Have you talked to your neighbor?
Sign on her lawn keeps you from hearing her?
Is it blue, is it red?

Truth is color blind.

Open your mind
and you may even find
you were saying the same thing
this whole time;
just lost in translation—
lost in emotion—
blinded by devotion to an idea.

We have the gift of expression
yet we use such discretion
for fear of rejection.
It's worth the connection – I tell you.
It's worth it.

TRAVELER

You didn't know me, but we looked the same.
Two ramblers down this road
much too uncanny to explain.

Necks curving downward, no pep in our spines.
I never shook your hand, friend,
though we were born of similar minds.

I beg you, weary traveler,
I beg you, rest your head
so I may do as you do
void of worry, void of dread.

YOUR RECEIPT, MA'AM

A smile is free;
priceless to those who need
a little boost this afternoon.

Don't fake it
but embrace it
if you find something
that stirs it.

Bleakness is hard to shake off
but so easy to get to.
A goal is a pinnacle—
if it's clear you'll get through.

Change cannot happen
when things are so easy
but have peace in knowing
it's worth every penny—
for your thoughts.

Answer or listen
because every question
deserves some attention.

THERE IS ALWAYS MORE

I hear where you've been
I see where you are
and believe me, my words
do not come from afar;
I've been somewhere near
only some years ago
but the more I could see
the less I could know.

I love you,
whoever you are.

THE VEIL

Although you made a claim yesterday
it may not be accurate today.
Your ego can wait.
As information emerges
embrace convergence.
We all have our fears
but one thing should be clear:
Our souls need to hear
what is right, what is true.
We exhaust ourselves
with labels and veils
to appeal
to someone we don't know.

Science is the new God,
experts: the apostles—
but science was always meant
to be questioned;
as life is ever-changing
discoveries call for rearranging.
What becomes of a fact
if proven untrue?

It's up to you.

Be accepted by the people
who are more adrift than you are?
or step out of the box—
invest in the future.
Not the feel-goods of today
avoiding conflict to stay
what— happy?

Happiness is a feeling;
highs and lows always fleeting
but Peace is a state of being
and seeing that life is more than this.
We're presented challenges
to make us stronger
yet prefer the easier way out.

So we look around
for someone else to tell us what is
because we don't have time for this.
Gotta get to work
to buy overpriced plastic
but the reality is:

If we just accept what we hear
without questioning it ourselves
we will always be products
on a system of shelves
until we are empty shells
with no personality—
no humanity—
giving up the differences
that help us balance all this.

Never forget this is your home too;
your mind is your castle,
don't let it crumble.
On your stairs let them stumble
because you are stronger
than any lie that's left at your door.

THIS

This isn't white versus black
This isn't the patriarchy
This isn't the "Karens"
THIS could be malarky…?
But...
THIS is corruption
THIS is manipulation
THIS is "authorities" giving you a station
THIS is fear tactics
THIS is money
THIS is blind compliance
Do you think THIS is funny?
THIS is threats of violence
thoughts of someone else
THIS is the distraction
you give to yourself
THIS is a biased idea
THIS is control
THIS is turning around
while you were on a roll
THIS is a law being rearranged
THIS is a "temporary measure"
THIS is restraint
You'll be doing just fine
until THIS is your saint.

TALKING HEADS

Power suits
perfected speech patterns
choosy tales of woe
keep us thinking
they're the ones who know.

Such trust in mouths
line dancing with prompters
won't renounce their words
but point sinuous fingers.

Just doing their job
bringing the bacon home
without considering
the ramifications sewn
into the future of families
not just their own.

Can this be of the past?
It's about time we outgrew
this dependence on commands
at the expense of autonomy.

CONTRADICTION

When looking through history
we say "that was horrible"
but when we're up to bat
we just claim it is normal.

We can't see in ourselves
what we point out in others
and refuse to admit
when what's coming out mirrors

all the things that we judge
in the past and the present
can't hold up to our actions.
Why are we so incessant?

We are passively living
with a guise of contentment
but we'll eventually look back
with explicable resentment

towards ourselves
and our children
as we try to teach them
all the lies we've been voicing
were just temporary treatment

for our dislike of uprooting
things we thought were all well
making blinded assessments
to protect from ourselves.
We feed on cognitive dissonance
and we can't even tell
that the back of our minds
know these mistakes all too well.

But we won't communicate
we just discriminate
against our own intentions.
We don't like the sensations
as we're being misled
by our preconceived notions.

This battle inside
decays our inspiration
brings a lack of motivation.
We're so bored, yet impatience
will rule us until
our minds can be still
for just one moment.

Breathe.

AUTHORITY

I was taught to raise my hand
and ask permission to stand
so as I grew older
the habit was soldered
to believe I was lesser than.

INNOCENCE

Little butterfly,
rest your weary wings
as a delicate creature like you
can't handle these sorts of things.

INDEPENDENT

I failed the test
while all the rest
stayed standing
in the line.
      I ran away
           to chase the day
                and the highest tree
                     I climbed.

THE TRAGEDY

She used to play endlessly,
make discoveries of her own.
No one taught her how.

Then she got schooled
she followed rules
and can't remember now.

DEAR HOPE

I've got a friend named Hope;
my lucky charm.
She comes and goes as she pleases
but means me no harm.

Hold me in your arms—
I don't want to chase you down.
Unreliable one, keep me safe—
reach out, don't let me drown.

You're a ghost on a black lake.
Oh, Reflection! I need your solid state.
Tap my shoulder then evaporate.

NEXT GEN.

Blueprints
for children
like programming code.
Take advantage of innocence
so the plan can unfold.

SOFT

Cuddled and coddled
A delusion of love.
Compliments and praise
Versus coming on tough.

Why bring on dependence
To perform for idolatry?
What we need to grow
Is critique and honesty.

Labelling fears and fantasies
Not as selfish personality
But against classic normality
Celebrated as equality....

THE ILLUSION

Money works like magic
On the printing press
It appears out of nowhere
Pays for our house arrest

Advertised as generosity
We should know better than that
The debt clock keeps rising
While the birth rate falls flat

This isn't a gratuity
It's laced with ambiguity
Not alluding to the poverty
We're outlining for children

We need workers on the line
While ambition declines
We think everything is fine
Out of sight and out of mind

With every generation
Sovereignty has less relation
We pour into taxation
While our logic is on vacation

OZ

They say most accidents
happen close to home
and the greatest achievements
out of the comfort zone—
but sadly enough
we've become prone
to sitting around acquiring
gratification from our phones.

Playing victim to the masses
even though—
we avoid formulating
resolutions of our own.

As we collect our banners
our gold stars and pins
which we stick by our hearts
to hide what's within—
our credence, I must say
begins to wear thin
as this spray paint
can't keep pace
with our rusting tin.

H IDE
E VERY
M ORAL
P ROJECT

We don't need it.
We never did;
the plastic clothes
and plastic lids.
There are alternatives.

With money
in big factories
inventiveness
is choked
by profit margins.

ELECT

Though I love to have the choice,
it's unclear if it's mine to make,
for promises of outcomes
can be empty—

even fake.

THE PRESENT

Rip each other off
to make a living.
No concept of giving
unless a holiday says so.
Where do we go
from here?

THE FREE MARKET

The tomatoes are fresh here;
no chemicals, nothing filled with air,
no wax to make them shine.
Quality wins us over this time.

Mr. Quantity no longer sells;
we built immunity against his spells.

HERE, YOU COULD USE THIS.

So wasteful we are. So distasteful it is
to go through things as quick as we do.

If we hadn't the need ten years ago
how now can we find its value?

Holding on to objects, piled up and forgotten,
dusty 'til pawned off
to the next unwilling person.

WITH LOVE

Why is vintage so popular?
It reminds of a simpler time
when objects weren't mass-produced
to sell to all online.

Defects were embraced;
unique to the craftsman who cared—
but as *new* turns more affordable
we forget that he's even there.

Not understanding why we crave it
though the warmth is something we sense.
We can try to deny it
but the stores can't supply
what these handcrafted gems represent.

POTENTIAL

How much potential can a person have?
How many accomplishments fit into a lifetime?
How much is there to learn?

One could waste such moments on wonder—
but I would rather strive to find that end.

A TANGENT

Chaos.
Confusion.
Illusion.
Scrambling minds.
Melting butter—

A blue jay
watches as I write this poem.
A sense of calm from the bird.
I look back to my words for a second
and he is gone.

The moment does not last
as questions bubble up so fast.

I wish to follow him.

This is not what I meant to write
but circumstances changed mid-flight.

AVOIDANCE

Marbles
colors
chasing down the hill

while all else is still.

Pass by the
sunken mailbox,
turn to the main strip.
Wrinkled plastic
pebbles, glass.
Birds are silent today.
Eyes peer
through windows.
Watch the race,
don't participate.
Puddles
without reflection.
Tulips wonder why
all is shy.
Goodnight world—
let someone else
take your place.

WITHOUT

Clarity does not come from pixels.
Eyes become so fickle
while watching tiny boxes—
lost in lies and paradoxes.

Torpid thought becomes the norm—
not aware of thunderstorms
that rap nonstop at your window
while your body rests in limbo
and your brain leaks out your ears
as you mold into your fears.

Where can you find said clarity
if you buy into catastrophe?
This can be answered simply
if you chose to listen critically.

You should not buy into screens
without knowing what it means
to live without them for a day
and simply walk the other way.

RELAPSE

Hit by a thousand emotions at once.
All was well...
Here comes the punch.

Didn't think I'd see you again...
yet here you are,
my dearest, old friend.

BEMUSE

Should you retreat to ideology?
Right and wrong do not bend to identity.
No matter a given social status
Or the way *you* hold your head
If your pride rejects what *is*
Your moral compass starves instead.

IGNORance

Watch me stumble through the garden
'til the sky turns red and orange.
Regard the feather sweeping down
to perch atop my cherry nose.

Will the doors close right behind me
as I shrink into the keyhole?
Can I scurry with the mouse
that disappeared under the table?

Call my mother: "Reach out for me,
I have slipped into the darkness.
Who am I? Where am I headed?
Hold the net, be still. I promise."

Catch me falling down the spiral.
Hold on tight. I'm in denial.

DON'T TAKE MY WORD FOR IT

So let me get this straight:
We're still treating each other
like we're sick until proven healthy?

That's the world we want to live in?
Lock up the population
'cause we just give in—
no need for information?

Use those big numbers
instead of reliable stats?
Accurate percentages;
we do away with that.

Using terror
to cover our errors—
Heart rates up
so we think we're stuck.

No way out. We're so excited
for things to be normal
but we'll never really go back;
we've already given so much away.

Thinking we've saved the day.
Well, that's just what we say
to justify our behavior.

Outlined promises:
If you comply, you'll be free,
but that's not what liberty is.

That's an ultimatum, force, coercion.
We could make bets but none of us win.

Let's be honest with ourselves—
please! If I sneeze
it might just be allergies.
I'm not a disease.

I'm not out to get you;
I'm just trying to help you
see past your own nose
if you froze your whole life
'cause talking heads told you so.

What are your sources?
"Experts" on pedestals?
Peer reviewed articles?
Define peer: equal levels.
Same field, same interests—
How about devil's advocate?
Proving your proof only gets you so far.
Look to the opposite to compare—
Make the effort and you'll see what's there.

Am I being unfair?
I don't jump to conclusions
to fuel an illusion.
If I don't know, I don't try to prove it.
I'll take the time to delve in;
ask questions, make mistakes
and admit them.

But this is just a poem.
If it *is* a call to action
let it be to cease distractions.
Titles are barely a fraction
of what is needed
to necessitate a sanction.

Just use your own mind;
don't believe anything I say
...right away...
Find out for yourself.
You have the ability.

APPLY

You are the sole owner of your psyche.
Filter with philosophy to avoid corrosion.
Do not steer clear of suspect ideas;
rather, practice what is bona fide
and hold what is *not* in your back pocket.

WHILE YOU'RE AHEAD

Art is a place to fully get lost in;
a place for your thinking—
development and comparison.
But to ruminate long
may take meaning away
as the words from a song
can get lost in the haze.

Drum snares and bass
vibrate in your conscience
and could intoxicate
'til your clarity is minced.

The flashes of sounds
resonating together
could clash through the movie
then in you forever.

Come back to the art
when you need to get through—
but go now with your knowledge.
I bid you adieu.

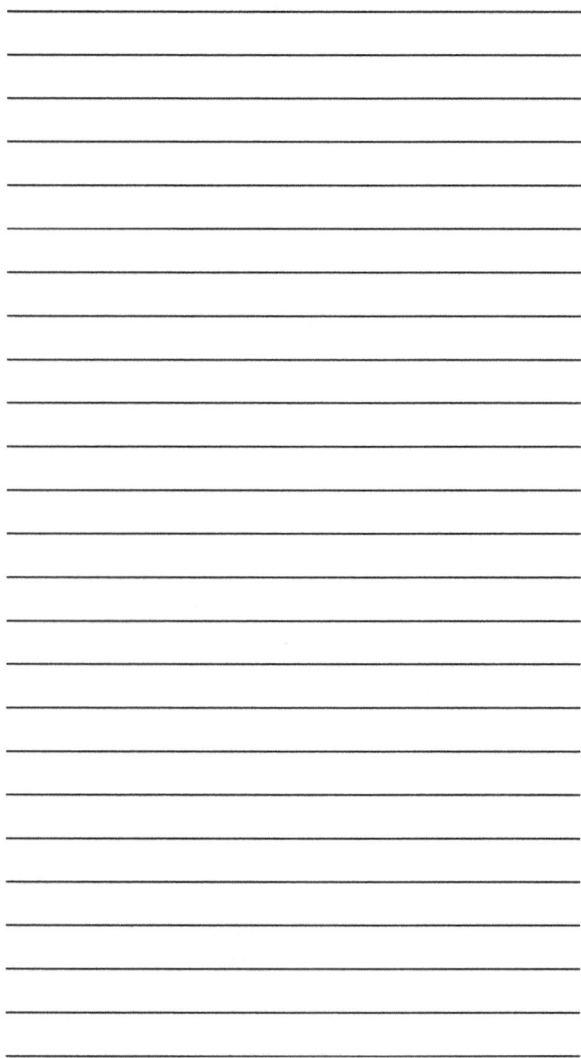

www.ingramcontent.com/pod-product-compliance
Lightning Source LLC
Chambersburg PA
CBHW021937040426
42448CB00008B/1106